Four Steps
to Manifest Anything

Four Steps to Manifest Anything

I have the POWER and so do YOU!

Workbook

Tami Friedman

To order additional copies of this book, contact:
Xlibris Corporation
1-888-795-4274
www.Xlibris.com
Orders@Xlibris.com
47408

Contents

I dedicate this book to my brother Craig.
I love you and pray for you.

Love Always
Your Sister

Congratulations! You are on your way to living the life of your dreams.

I have compiled four simple steps to manifest any vision as long as it is for the good of all involved. Your dreams and highest goals are usually the heart's desire and God's will for us. What we are seeking is also seeking us.

So let's begin the process.

Introduction

Before I had income real estate properties, a series 7 and 63 on Wall Street, and miracles working in my life, I was at the lowest point in my entire life. I remember feeling so afraid of not having enough food or money to cover my rent or living expenses for the month. I realized my worst fear and not only was the money not available to me but I was also very depressed and unable to function in the work place. I was at the bottom and this is exactly when I was able to learn how to work with my mind, other people, and the universe. I want to share this with you because it saved my life. We all have different roads available to us and if you are reading this book, I wish you all the wonderful miracles that I have been so gratefully blessed with.

Sending you much love and light.

I Have The Power And So Do You!

Four Steps to Manifest Anything: A Simple Guide to Manifest the Goals You Desire.

My book is a self-help manual for applying spiritual principles to achieve success in all areas of our lives. When I was 27 years old, my world fell apart. I had started my own company, was making $100,000 a year, and through ill-advised business advice, I lost all my money and was living hand to mouth. This could have been a disaster, instead it taught me the secrets of turning around a negative situation. I was unable to function in the workplace due to an incurable chronic illness known as fibromyalgia and severe depression.

I wrote this book because I want to free others from limiting beliefs that have held them back from achieving their full potential. Since I have been diagnosed with clinical depression and fibromyalgia, a difficult illness, I work on myself daily for healing.

Similar to such classics as Shakti Gawain's *Creative Visualization* and Marsha Sinetar's *Do What You Love and the Money Will Follow,* my book demonstrates how to achieve practical results using spiritual tools. The success of the newest phenomena, *The Secret,* certainly shows the power of this market.

In *Four Steps to Manifest,* I detail how to define one's goal, clear the way, take action and then sit back and be receptive to accomplishment. I use examples from my own life, quotes from others who have overcome great hardships and easy to apply techniques.

I believe the strongest reason why *Four Steps to Manifest Anything* is different from other titles in the self-help spiritual field is because even though it is a short book (less than 107 pages), it offers a blueprint by which an individual can change their lives in 90 days.

I am now living my dreams of living on a horse property in New York State. I live off my real estate investments and I am also writing books, i.e., Real Estate Rich, Young and Spiritual.

You are a perfect being.

God Loves You.

You were created in perfection,

By perfection,

For perfection.

Your success is guaranteed.

Please write the date that you started in this workbook.

_____ Date

_____ Signed

Some Points of my Philosophy

We are each responsible for all of our experiences. Every thought we think is creating our future. The most powerful place for change to occur is in the present moment.

It takes a second to change our entire life. When we really love ourselves, everything in our life works.

Chapter 1

To Dream the Vision

Starting with Step One. The first step is a dream and a vision. Before we can do anything, whenever anything is created, it always starts with a dream, a vision. We imagine our creation. *Please allow yourself the next 30 days to work on the first step.*

Everything that happens in the universe, on the planet, in our lives, in our reality, is first a thought. There are some theories that say the first thing that ever happened was a sound, but in our reality as humans living on the planet and living in the material world, it is a thought first. It can become a manifestation, but it has to start with a thought.

There are only four steps in this entire book on manifesting. I was going to say the first is the most important, but each step is the most important because without any one step, I believe it's not possible to manifest. So I think each step is just as important as the next. Identifying the dream and the vision is the first and the most important step. And I'm going to say that about each of the steps, that it is the most important step!

So how does one know what their vision is? It would probably be a good question to explore. The way to find that is to look within and find out things that we love about life, things that we love about ourselves, about other people, about causes, possibly animals, the environment, possibly an art form or creative project. I suggest writing in a journal. I like to do treasure mapping as well, but we'll get to that soon. First write a journal and keep notes on the things you like to do, what makes you feel really good inside. And really look at what you think you should be by what society dictates, because that is *not* it. Look deeper at what you want.

It's really important to look at those things because many of us have been working on them our whole lives—becoming teachers or doctors or lawyers or whatever the profession might be because we thought we should do that, or because someone else thought we should do that. But maybe it's not what we have in our heart so it's not our real vision. It's just our work. And we can become successful at our vision as well. You know, there are books such as, "Do What You Love and the Money Will Follow" and other books of that nature, and I totally agree with them. Because the first step is to find out what it is exactly—who you are—what you want—why you're here—what's your purpose.

There are other ways to find a vision. I like to do treasure maps. They're really fun, like an arts and crafts project. It reminds me of going to public elementary school. You cut out magazine pictures and you paste them into a collage and you have this fun project at the end of the day. If we do this on a more spiritual level, on a conscious level of manifesting, not only is it fun but it's very effective. So the next step I would suggest if someone is not clear what their vision is, to go ahead and start collecting magazines, books, articles, symbols, things that you love, things that are things you want to have, things that you would like to work toward and things that you only wish and dream that you could ever possibly have.

This involves taking a couple of hours of time, and sitting down at a table and going through magazines and looking for the house that you like, and the relationship that looks like the kind you are looking for, with the type of love or the type of connection or communication with an individual that you are seeking. And possibly find some scenery like travel, places you'd like to go or places you'd like to live. Put all of this on your treasure map.

Also it's very important to put into our treasure map some kind of spiritual center, and I say center because I think it does belong in the center. And I don't really have an opinion as to what that would be. Everybody has their own individual higher power. It could be God, it could be Buddha, it could be Allah, it could be Jesus, it could be the Universe, it could be good positive energy, or it could be a group of people that are your support group. As long as it's a force and it's bigger than you are, it's a place to start in terms of a higher power. I think this belongs in the center of our treasure map to give us the support and inspiration we need to go along the way. So cut out pictures relating to that as well.

The fun thing about treasure mapping is that you can dream big. There's no "must" and there's no "have to" and there's no deadline and there's no guideline. This is all you and your imagination and creativity, and your dream and your vision of what you would love—love, love, love—in your life. So I want you to dream big. That's really important. When it comes to setting goals and achieving goals, that's a whole other story. But when it comes to treasure mapping, be big, be bold, and be everything you've ever wanted to be, and put it on paper.

At my two day seminar held in upstate New York we take special care in developing our visions. The goal is to have our true desire manifest so our dreams become reality.

You'll find as you're doing this, your vision opens up and grows with you as you're putting pictures in. You'll find that, "Oh, yeah, not only do I want a house like that, but I also want a summer retreat. And not only do I want one income property but I want three. And not only do I want a marriage but I want a loving, wonderful, healing, nurturing relationship." So you'll be growing with your vision as you go through this process. And I invite you and allow you to grow big as you explore this. Please think big, but also stay grounded in reality.

The third way of coming to discover our vision and dream is to meditate. Ask ourselves questions such as, "If money wasn't a factor . . . if time wasn't a factor . . . if age wasn't a factor . . . if there were no factors holding me back, what would I love to be doing right now in my life? What would my life look like? How would I be in the world? What would that look like?" And I would suggest doing this in a quiet place where you can relax and breathe and allow yourself to just fall into this state of vision and dream without the world coming in, and you know, worrying about the phone ringing or the bill that wasn't paid or the person you had an argument with. Get all of that out of the equation for now, just for now, just for this aspect of it. We're creating a dream and a vision, and it's really important to get it as clear as possible so we know what our heart is telling us.

This is something that I think a lot of people don't allow themselves to do because it's scary. It's scary because what if we never, ever achieve it? And so if we never discover what it is we want and we never achieve it, that's no great loss. But I think once we discover what it is that we want, then it becomes scary. Now, what if I don't get it? It's out there. At this point when you discover your visions, negativity will come up big time. Do not discuss the vision with every person that you come into contact with, or even people who are close in your life because this is really a precious part of the manifesting. Take yourself seriously and treat yourself like a special gem. These early stages are the most important and precious. Please treat them like that.

In the early stages of conception of an idea it's so fragile. It can easily be dispelled, broken down, disintegrated, and it's so important to nourish this, to protect this, to develop this and to hold it sacred in our own soul and heart. And if we feel the need to share, share only with people that we feel are very safe and who are also in the same process of working on visions and working on things that they would love to do in their life.

It's very easy for someone to say, "Why would you want to do that?" because they would then have to look at their own vision if they were going to support yours. So it's really important that you realize when you're going through this process to find very supportive people who are also working on manifesting their vision.

I have some suggestions on getting support. If you don't have support in this area already, there are so many places to go. First of all, there are twelve step groups that are free, and they deal with manifesting money, abundance and vision. A good one is D.A. which is the Debtors Anonymous program, that addresses self-debting and not taking care of ourselves on the level of nurturing our dreams and goals. They will help you get on track with your money and help you find your way through the steps.

There are also life coaches, success coaches, people who are trained to specifically help you work on your goals and attain and achieve your goals. Now, this is a paid service but it's also much more individualized and it's a bigger luxury to give to yourself to have a personal coach to work with you along the way. And I would recommend if you're going this route to interview a few different coaches and find out the person that you feel a good chemistry with, that you feel that you could bounce off ideas and it just flows really well with this other individual. That might be the coach that you'd want to work with. I'm not a big believer in credentials. I'm more on who this person is, what they've achieved in their life, how you connect with them. If you have a good sense and a good intuition that they could help you, then you've found a good coach for yourself. I invite you to work with me one-on-one if you so choose. Contact the staff at www.Ihavethepower.us.

There is other support available. We can find action partners, and these would be similar to a support group, but what you do is find a partner, a friend, a work buddy, a relative, someone who will fit into the "safe" category of people to share with, for starters. It would be someone who is also walking this walk, working toward attaining their life goals and visions. And this could be your action buddy, who will support you as you manifest your vision.

Just getting back to the creation part of the vision, although I'm suggesting getting support, I firmly believe that when you're establishing your vision, this is done in solitude. This is done between you and your higher self in quiet, meditative time, in space that's created safely for yourself to explore. This is a place where you do not want outside influences. Once you've established what it is, then as stated before, you bring in the safe people as the next part of the vision/dream process.

I want to talk for a second about myself and my own experience of vision. I've had many different visions in my life through different times of my life. Some I've achieved and some I have not achieved. And sometimes I've achieved them and had success with them and then found that there's a new vision that was very apparent. At other times I'd go through a phase of time when I didn't know what my vision was and I was kind of lost for a little while. These are all okay places to be. I just want you to know that it's an ongoing process of co-creating and manifesting with the universe. It's not a one-time job. It's ongoing, it's a life fulfilling deal that we have with the universe that we are co-creators.

So I'll give you an example of some of the things I've done, and how I knew they were visions. When I was quite young, I had two big desires. One of them was to be a veterinarian because I loved animals. And I loved taking care of them and I would find strays on the street, bring them home, so I thought being a veterinarian would be a great thing for me. I also had a love and passion for style and fashion, beauty and looking good, drawing, and artistic endeavors involving color, fashion sense and style.

It's interesting in life how things work out because I had these visions at a very young age. I was 12-13 years old, and the way that life dealt the cards for me, I was out of my parents' house at age 16. I'd graduated from high school at 15 years old, but I wasn't able to be supported by my family and go to college at the same time, so I knew that veterinary school was out of the question, and I'd have to go to Plan B.

That put me in fashion because I was able to get a job in the fashion industry at 16 years old and also go to night school at F.I.T. and work toward the vision I had for fashion design. Sometimes the world shows us what to do next. It's not just all our own effort. We need to be guided along a little bit as well, and we need to be open to the signs. But we also have to have a clear intent of what we want first, and then the world shows us where we are going.

So this is an example of two visions I had at a young age, and how one manifested and one didn't, and why. Also I just want to account for myself a little bit to say how I feel qualified (for lack of a better word) to be writing on this subject. As someone who has been called an expert in the field, although humbly I don't feel like an expert in the field, I do acknowledge this. I know that I have been working spiritually with the universe and other people for many years and I've seen certain trends and patterns and how they work.

I've also done a serious amount of inside work, spiritually, emotionally, and self-help-wise, through other healers and motivators. I've worked with my own coaches, and I continue to listen to such people as Wayne Dyer and Caroline Myss, and Tony Robbins, to mention a few. And it's a continuous thing. But the reason I feel qualified to talk about this is because I've been working with this myself for many years and I've seen it work in my life. So that's why I feel that I will share this and can share this with you. And I firmly believe that anybody reading or listening to this book at this time can have what they want, as well, if they do all four steps to the best of their ability, and if their desires are for the highest good.

As we approach more clarity in our vision, the voices of doubt and fear will become so much louder than ever, because the part of us which is scared that this will never happen is terrified now, because we're identifying exactly what it is we want. So now this is a crucial step, although we're going into the next step and I said the first step was the most important, but this second one is the most important step, too. ***This is the step of removing obstacles.***

Chapter 2

To Remove the Obstacles

The reason that this is a very important step is because if we allow the obstacles to block us, we will not have our vision. If we remove the obstacles and change our belief system, we are on our way to having our vision manifest. So at this point, it's critical to start listening to what our head is telling us, and not believing it, but just listening. Slow down and listen to our negative thinking—I promise you it is there.

There are many different ways of doing this. The first thing that I like to do is to write out what the fears are. Whatever the goal is, or the dream or the vision, that's fine, but immediately after that comes the fear. "Oh, I can't afford it," or "I'm too old," or "I'm not smart enough," or "That will never happen for me," or "If I do this something bad will happen," or "I was told as a young child I could never do something like this." Whatever those obstacles, fears, thoughts, and negative beliefs are they need to be put on paper. That would be the first thing.

So now that you have your vision, we're in Chapter Two now, writing out our negative beliefs. I like to list them also, so we can be very clear about what we believe is *not going to happen—or is going to happen—from a negative standpoint.* And it's important to get this stuff out because it's in our heads. So if it's in our heads, it's in the conscious, the subconscious and the unconscious, and it will be in our lives if we don't get it out. Our beliefs determine our success. This is why at my two day seminar we devote a great deal of time to developing a more positive belief system.

I like to look at the mind like a computer. We have to delete something and then we have to put something in. You find a sentence—whatever that negative belief is or that fear is, and as it's coming up, the best way to do this is to write immediately when that thought comes into mind. Like, "Who do you think you are? You can't do that." Isolate it and stop. Stop the tape right here. Delete. That's an old thought. My new thought is, "I can absolutely have what I want and desire. I'm a child of God, and I can manifest great and wonderful things in my lifetime." It's good to do that on a regular basis but it's great to do that when it's actually happening your life. Exactly when the thought comes up is when it's most powerful and if you delete it and put in something else, it's gone. You've cleared it. But if you keep just putting in the positive, putting in the positive, and waiting to change the negative it will eventually disappear, but it's not immediate. It's a repetitive job of listening and then saying, "Stop, change that belief."

And it takes a lot of work to isolate a thought. We're so used to believing our thinking, and we have a lot of different thoughts, so we just believe whatever feeling that comes over us. We could be in a depressed mood or an angry state or a sad state—or even in an elated state where we're focusing on some kind of addictive behavior or obsessive thought. So to isolate the thoughts that go into the feelings is a job. It takes work and it's very well-worth doing this work. That's one way to remove obstacles.

Let's use an example of someone wanting to lose weight. Let's say their goal is to lose 30 pounds and to fit into a certain size dress, and to be at a fitness level where their energy is high. At this point, what their mind would probably be saying is, "That'll never happen for you. You're not cut out to be like that. You have big bones. You have a different metabolism. You're much slower than other people. Other people can do it, but you can't do it." All B.S. Yes, you can.

Now this is exactly what is *not* to be believed but what needs to be looked at. We need to know what the enemy is and what the sabotage is so that we know what we're dealing with. So it's really important for this step, to write it down on paper, exactly the way your mind is telling you. If your mind is telling you, "Oh, I'm too fat, I'll never lose weight," write this down. If your mind is telling you, "That is not what my content is made of, my metabolism is different," write that down. If your mind is telling you, "You're not smart enough. You didn't finish college. Who do you think you are?" write that down.

Do *not* believe the negativity—change the belief to a positive, like "I am smart enough."

The negative thought is not true, but it is in your head and you could make it true by believing it. So right now we're in the process of removing obstacles by identifying them first. At this stage of the process, of the four steps, I think it's critical to start looking for an action buddy, a life coach, a success coach, possibly a therapist if the feelings are very intense, and to start looking at who would be a supportive person in your life to help you work through this stuff, because this is probably where you're going to need more support than in any of the other steps.

This is because we tend to believe what our minds tell us, and we're going to need a reality check from someone else other than ourselves, who is honest and safe and trustworthy. So if you already have an action partner, a therapist, a twelve step group, a buddy, or even a best friend who you totally trust because they're going through this process, then this is useful. If you don't have one at this time, I suggest you continue to do the writing, but it's a serious place to start looking for support in your life around this issue. Please feel free to call me for help in finding someone to work with you.

The most important ingredient to any success is first and foremost, the belief that something can be done. Without this very first step the idea or goal is only a dream or a fantasy. Once the thought comes to mind that maybe this is possible, at this point it is critical to check out our beliefs around the idea so that we know what we are up against and we can then create an action list.

As a life coach this is my job. I help people move past their own blocks. When a client decides to work toward a goal there are usually obstacles along the way but some we have more control over than others. I like this part of the coaching process because it's very basic. You either believe something or you don't, and to uncover this trail of thoughts is the road map to change and success.

My favorite teacher, coach and motivational speaker is Anthony Robbins. He is brilliant, powerful and sometimes very radical in his approach. An example is his technique called NAC (neuro-associated conditioning). Robbins realized that in order to change a belief we first need to know that we have it (neuro). Second we need to interrupt the pattern by doing something different at the exact time the thought pattern is present, in other words, think of something different that you want to associate with this train of thought. Last, he determined that in order for change to take place we need to condition this association over and over until we associate the thought with this new condition. Robbins will do this in one session with a one-on-one client or at a workshop. The only problem with working with him is that he's very expensive and it is very difficult to get an appointment with him because of his heavy schedule.

You can, however, do the work yourself or with a life coach, friend or mentor. When I coach my clients I like to use some of Robbins' strategy along with other techniques such as positive reinforcement methods I learned while becoming certified as a Hypnotherapist. Working with people and their blocks is sometimes quite a challenge. People must be ready to give up an old idea in order to install a new one. You can't have fear and faith at the exact same time so it's where you must let go of one in order to have the other. If someone wanted to hand me a gift, I could not hold it if my hands were already full. Something would have to go. I like to look at the mind and all of the beliefs in it as I would look at a computer. As we all know if we don't clear out some junk, things don't work as well, and sometimes we can't even move at all. The same way that we scan our computers for viruses and obsolete information we need to do to ourselves every so often. In twelve step programs this is a fourth step which is very important in the recovery process. In life it is a personal inventory, deleting the old and replacing it with better and more efficient beliefs.

This is where change starts to happen right at the moment when we can give up our old programming for a new and better idea that will move us toward our goals.

I would have to say that this is the step, this is the place where most people get off the journey towards self healing by saying, "I really don't want to do that anyway," and give themselves a million reasons and rationalizations why they really, really don't want to have this manifest for them. It's a great place to rationalize. It's the biggest deceiver of the truth that we'll ever have on this planet and it's in our own heads. Please do *not* give up before the miracles happen for you, because they will.

I would just like to tell everyone at this point that you are so fabulous, that you don't even know how fabulous you are, because most people have not gotten past this particular step which is removing the obstacles and the blocks which are the things that tell us we are so not fabulous, we are so not qualified, we are so not self-sufficient. And this is the place where people often lose it. *And I'm here to tell you that you are great and you are qualified, you are wonderful, you are brilliant, creative, artistic, articulate, magnificent and fabulous, ready, able and willing to create and co-create with the universe.*

It's funny because I speak with a lot of people about their childhood, and I don't know many that come from a childhood where they've been nurtured and told that they were fabulous and really walk away with a very high self-worth and self-esteem, because we're basically a very dysfunctional society. And I think we're all moving into this stage of discovering and exploring the abilities that we have as humans, abilities that we previously had no clue about but that we are realizing now we can develop and work with, beyond our five senses.

We weren't taught this as children. Our parents weren't taught this. I think that thousands of years ago, they possibly did have a clue to some of this stuff. They knew that they existed, but they realized they didn't know anything else. Thus the major religions and works of history in different societies and civilizations grew out of this search for answers. Have we stopped searching? I think today we think we know so much that we lose sight of what we need to see. We already think that we know it, or we think it's impossible. In any event we are controlling our thought processes.

And that's the difference between ours and the civilizations prior, because other earlier civilizations knew that they didn't have all the answers. They knew that were clueless, so they were so much more open to the possibilities of new ideas.

I'm going to think about this for a minute. What if we lived on a planet or at a time or in a society where all people had a very high level of self worth and self-esteem, and we all loved our lives, and we were all living exactly the way we wanted to, and creating and co-creating with the universe, and feeling self-complete? Could you just even imagine that for a minute, the kind of planet that we'd be living on? It would be absolutely beautiful and full of love.

It's kind of mind-blowing to even go there for a second, because first of all, it's never existed in the society as we know it. There's always been the yin and yang, all the different dichotomies. But just to think of it for a second, if we were all vibrating on that level, where we'd be as a species, as a society, as a planet? Where would we go from there? How far could we take that? And I think it's just amazing because that could happen.

If you know someone who is already acting with this consciousness, someone who has achieved the goal you have identified for yourself, you can use this tool for of removing obstacles called modeling. Tony Robbins uses it a lot in Neuro Linguistic Programming (NLP) teaching. It's called modeling because it's modeling behavior after people who have actually achieved the same goal. So acting as if until it becomes is like acting your way into good thinking.

An example of that might be choosing friends who are very successful, and because you're around people with that energy all the time, eventually that energy gets into your own mind. It's kind of like contagion or osmosis. Call it what you like but it's acting as if until it becomes true.

Another way to remove obstacles is praying, and this is a helpful tool. My own experience with it is, when I was younger I was brought up atheist or agnostic. I really didn't have a spiritual foundation at home. I was born into a family. We did traditional stuff, but there was no real connection with a higher force, so I really didn't have that tool of praying or asking for help from God, the universe or any other source.

I found, though, as I did become more spiritual and have now achieved a certain belief system, that when I call upon that energy to help me with my actions and behaviors and direction, it's a force that works with me, and it's wonderful, and it's a fantastic tool. I can't even tell you how fantastic. The thing is you do it. You pray and ask for help in removing the obstacles, the character flaws, the defects, the fear, or to help you achieve the highest good for all concerned because our highest desire is usually the will of the universe, as well. So if we ask for that help, we usually are guided with that.

The interesting thing about prayer is that we don't really have control over it. We put it out there, we ask for help, and then we have to just let go. We have to just let go of the thoughts around it, the attachment to the "When is it going to happen?" and then just to trust that it will happen. And that's the best way to utilize that tool of prayer—to ask for the help, pray for the help, and pray for whether it's in the highest good of all concerned, and then let it go. Do something else. Preoccupy yourself with some behavior that's good for you, that's nurturing, and do *not* concentrate on that thought any longer.

Another wonderful tool for removing negativity, fear and obstacles is to build and maintain and achieve self-esteem by doing small, esteem-filled actions on a regular basis until they become a natural practice in your daily life. Bubble baths are wonderful, getting massages, facials, taking care of what you eat, having yourself on a really good, nutritious food plan, exercising, making sure your body feels good, and making sure you're in tune with nature. Feeling good on a regular basis is very, very helpful in removing obstacles and negative beliefs because you're adding self-esteem and you're adding nurturing actions which leave less room for negative actions and beliefs. Also doing good deeds for someone else promotes this self-esteem and well being.

As I said earlier, support groups are very important and helpful as long as they're safe. So find people who are working on a path similar to the one you're working on. Not necessarily exactly the same goal or dream, but working on a spiritual path to achieve and manifest their goals and dreams. Because people who are on the same path will realize how important and valuable your work is, they might be more sensitive to the information and the tools you're working with and to your feelings. These are the safe people who can give you support.

This is one of my favorite tools—*volunteering*. Do something of service to help others. It is such a great tool by taking ourselves out of whatever negativity is in our heads and putting some positive thoughts and self-esteem in their place. By valuing our time and our actions, we see how we help and are continuing to help others. It's wonderful how giving brings everything full circle on a 360 degree turn. It's karmic: what goes around comes around!

I like this one, too. Get clear, which means when something is bothering you, look at it. Dissect it. Figure out what it is so you won't be obsessing on it. It could be, for example, that you're obsessing about money—fear of not having enough. What if this, what if that? Get clear. Look at your money. Balance your checkbook. Know exactly what you need. The more precise you are with the universe, the more clearly you can ask for what it is you want. You need to know exactly what you need or want before you can ask for it.

Another very important tool here is to take *responsibility*. So another "R" in the "Removal" of obstacles is "Responsibility." When we own up to our own behavior, we release part of our mind and energy that's attached to that behavior. And it's amazing because it's just the opposite of what we think we're doing with it. For instance, we may feel guilty about something we said to someone. Instead of just ignoring it and saying, "Oh, it's okay," if we take responsibility, pick up the phone, write a letter, confront that person and say, "You know what? My behavior at that time was something less than what I would like it to be. And I just want to affirm and I just want to say that I acknowledge that, I admit it, I'm sorry for that and I would like to have said something different." By doing that you take away the energy in your mind that was attached to that negativity.

And you could then use that energy for good, positive healing and manifesting.

I love this one. Just be mindless once in awhile. Take a bicycle ride. Go pick flowers. Have fun. Go out and skip, jump. Go horseback riding. Call up a friend and do something silly. Go see a movie that you wanted to see, or see an old movie again. Go to a play, a concert. Take yourself out for a really fun meal. Take yourself out on a date. Dress up and go someplace that you really want to go.

If we practice even some of these tools in our 90-day period, in our 90 days of the Four Steps to Manifest, we will see results beyond our wildest dreams. Reach out to other people that are in need, not necessarily support. Maybe it's nothing you need from them, but something they need from you. It's kind of like service but it's not a volunteer job. It's just reaching out to give a hand to another human on a path. If you see someone struggling with something, open the door for them, help them, make a phone call, or send a card. Just reach out. Even smiling on a regular basis with other people allows good energy in and releases negativity.

Find out a little about *Feng Shui* and look at the areas in your house that may be clogged or lacking in the energy that you might prefer. Maybe get a book from the library or buy a book on Feng Shui or just read a column on Feng Shui. There are a couple of recommended Feng Shui books on my website that are just helpful tools. Maybe you can add certain colors in areas of your house that represent the love area, that represent the fame and fortune area, success or spiritual area. There are things that you can do to enhance your living space. So Feng Shui is really a wonderful tool because it creates harmony and positive feelings via color and energy.

Let go of ego. This is a really important step in general. To live a humble life—and I'm not talking in terms of humble where you don't have things or you're less fortunate than others. I mean humble in the way that you are a human among humans, and you could have whatever you want as long as you're helping and fulfilling your purpose on the planet. So removing ego is part of the Removal process. Part of the removing of ego is also accepting and become aware of the fact that we do not—and I'll repeat, *we do not*—have all the answers. We do not know everything. We may think we know a lot because our ego tells us that we know everything we need to know. But when we surrender to the universe or a higher power, we realize we're just a player among players, an actor in the play of life. We're just a worker among workers. We're part of the scheme, the big picture. *We are not* the big picture. We're part of the big picture, and when we get that, we remove our ego. And when we remove our ego, we're open to information from others and the universe. We're then teachable.

There are thousands or maybe even millions of books written on how to change, how to self-help, how to achieve something. The ones that I have been listening to and the ones that I truly believe work are on a list of suggested reading on my website if you want to check it out. I start with Neuro Linguistic Programming, which describes the same principles that I'm talking about. NLP is about examining our belief system, accepting our belief system and deleting the negative belief and putting in a positive belief to replace the old one.

I don't think it's possible to just listen to a tape or take a pill. It's something we need to do on a regular basis until we change the system. As we saw before, we have to delete the negative thoughts from our brain, our computer, so that there will be new space to put in positive thoughts. We need to unclog it from these thought patterns that are holding us down, weighing us down, keeping us cluttered with information that is not helpful and basically hurtful. So it's part of the system.

In talking about all of the different systems and beliefs and books and theories on change, there is no instant fix. It's something that we need to grab by the reins, look at and work with. This is the work, and that's why it's called work.

Please allow another 30 days to work on Step 2.

Chapter 3

To Take Actions

Step Three is about taking actions, so we're going to talk a little bit about actions. This is more like, you know, basically a technical, black and white, A to Z, do 1 through 5 today. Some people suggest that people take 10 actions toward their vision on a regular basis. I think that's a lot in the beginning. I think if someone takes three actions per day toward their vision, they will start manifesting things pretty quickly. So I think that we should start with three actions per day for the first three weeks, and then after three weeks, you could take up to six actions a day.

Actions could be anything from making a phone call, returning a phone call, placing an ad, doing research, writing, or designing. Whatever the vision or goal is, the actions would be according to that. So it's just implementing and putting them into action, putting them into plan, putting them out in the universe, taking the necessary steps to have things happen. This is more of a doing step, an action step, as opposed to the other ones which are meditative or spiritual or introspective.

Handbooks, guide books, etc. I also want to recommend in this action chapter, a kind of book that's sold in nearly every bookstore, the Idiot's Guide to . . . . A book like this will offer basic principles to take one step at a time in achieving a goal, and that would be great to use in coordination with the goal you have in the action chapter.

The action step is also where I would totally suggest for people to get a life coach to work with them, to get a therapist possibly to work with them. I don't know if a therapist is the proper person in this case but sometimes it is. It helps to have a support group possibly to work with on this step, because sometimes it just helps to report in on a regular basis. Here is a tool called book-ending. You report your actions for the day in the morning, and then later when the day is complete, report back to that same person and acknowledge that the actions were taken during that day. It really helps to check in those two times in a day with someone who's supportive to make sure you take the actions.

Another action may be to hire a consultant or a specialist in the field in which you want to achieve the goal or desired outcome. So research could be one action in that case, and then actually hiring someone to work by the hour to implement the strategy is also a form of taking action. Finding a mentor is also wonderful, and having coffee or conversations on a regular basis with the mentor is another action. You can compare their experience and strength with you regarding a similar vision, not the same, but a similar vision in which they've already had success.

This goes back to what I mentioned in Chapter Two. It's what Neuro Linguistic Programming (NLP) calls modeling, when we find someone who we'd call a mentor, someone who we'd call a role model in a certain area, and doing what they do, and living the way they live, and acting like they act.

Two examples I'll use from my own experience are, when I first became a life coach in 1996, I hired a life coach to work as my coach so that she could help me along and, if you will, to model her behavior and what she does. So I could work hands-on and see how that works. And secondly, when I put my website together, I hired a consultant, someone who does this for a living and has their own website and helps others build their own websites. I just took one step at a time, one action at a time to get it all together. So this could illustrate the action state.

And I also want to say all along throughout this book that these steps continually take place. It's not like you do the step and you're done. If you do the step, you work on the next step, and then you might have to go back to the first step because you need to redefine or refine a visualization or you might need to take more actions in one day, or you might need to meditate more in one day or allow more. So you use all the four steps all the time.

In the action step, find a way to bring a spiritual practice into your life on a daily basis. As for me, to use my experience for a minute, I've been meditating on a daily basis in a Tibetan Buddhist fashion, and I find it to be extremely helpful in just allowing the dharma, or the Buddhist information and the Buddhist teachings, into my world and into my life, first thing in the morning. I'm just allowing the goodness in. I don't judge or suggest or recommend any one particular practice. If something works for you, that's great. If it's Buddhism, great. If it's Kabalah, it's fine. If it's Christ consciousness, that's fine too. Whatever it is, as long as it's all good energy and it brings you empowerment and makes you feel lighter, happier and more energized, then I would say you're on the right track. The important feeling is peace, peace of mind.

Praying every morning is an action. Writing in your journal every day is an action. Making calls to get more information about visions are actions. Putting together a business plan or doing research are also actions.

Continue to take actions three times a day for the next 30 days. You will see great results.

Chapter 4

To Allow the Universe to Co-Create With Us

Step Four is probably the most overlooked step. In fact, when I've looked in many books to research allowing, they don't have it. They have acceptance, abundance, affirmation, belief system, creative visualization, manifesting, etc. They have many different aspects of manifesting, but the *allowing* part is very seldom heard. And to start off this chapter, I want to read something on attachment to goals.

I'm quoting from Shakti Gawain's book "Reflections in the Light":

"July 1. Attachment to Goals. If you have a great deal of attachment to a particular goal, it may interfere with your ability to manifest it. Often when there is a strong attachment to something, there is a great deal of fear underneath. Fear of not getting what we want. It is perfectly okay to creatively visualize something to which you have a lot of attachment. If it doesn't work out, realize that your own inner conflict may be sending out conflicting messages. Relax and accept your feelings. Understand that resolving your inner conflict is probably an important part of growth. It's a wonderful opportunity to look more closely at your own attitude about life." And the visualization is: "*I relax and accept my feelings.*"

I'm going to read a quote out of the *Daily Wisdom Book*. It consists of 365 Buddhist inspirations, edited by Mark Bartok. Another morning meditation.

"May 3. Every minute you perform hundreds of karmic actions, yet you are hardly conscious of any of them. In the stillness of meditation, however you can listen to your mind, the source of all this activity. You learn to be aware of your actions to a far greater extent than ever before. This self-awareness leads to self control, enabling you to master your karma rather than to be mastered by it."

And here's another one from the same book:

"November 12. Non-attachment doesn't mean that you get rid of your spouse. It means you free yourself from wrong views about yourself and your spouse. Then you find that there's love there, but it's not attached. It's not distorting, clinging and grasping. The empty mind is quite capable of caring about others and loving in a pure sense of love, but any attachment will always distort that."

And that's about, again, attachment as opposed to allowing. I have two more quotes about meditation from *Daily Wisdom.*

"November 1. A teacher is essential. If you were to buy a Rolls Royce, and instead got all the parts of the car and an instruction manual on how to assemble it, you'd panic. What's this? Where's my car? You would need someone to show you how to put it together. It's the same with meditation. We need someone to show us how to put everything together inside our minds.

"November 2. While meditating we are bound to find ourselves carried away by trains of thought. When we recognize that this has happened, we may react with frustration, disappointment or restlessness. All such responses are a waste of time." Just make a mental note, stop, and start again. It's that simple. No reason to complicate matters.

Not only are we allowing the good, the light, the universe, the forces that work with us to help us manifest and co-create, we are also uninviting influences that we do not want. And I want to just quote a short prayer called Babaji's Uninvited Influence Prayer. I think it's good to know because all forces are not with us, and not everything is light and good, so I just think it's important to affirm that, as well, to allow only the force that's going to work with us.

So here's Babaji's Uninvited Influence Prayer:

"To all influences uninvited into my aura, I send love and light. You are whole and healed. You are each created as love and light.

You are still love and light. You each feel no pain and you are not afraid. You have a perfect place to go, and I ask that you go there now. Each of you go in peace. I close my aura to all except my higher self. I send all negative thought forms that may be around me, my body, my home, my children, my pets, my properties, my business, etc.—love and light."

So that's one prayer for the uninvited influences, and I also want to keep affirming the process of allowing. Allowing the dharma, allowing the good of the universe, allowing the Christ consciousness, allowing the teachings that we've taken in that are very healing to our souls, allowing ourselves to take those in, and to affirm that we do deserve and are willing to accept the highest good for all involved, ourselves and others. This usually comes at the same time as our vision because our vision is usually inspired by higher forces.

So it's usually working with us, as long as the vision is coming from a place of giving back, doing some type of service, sharing something, and it doesn't matter if you're going to make billions of dollars on the project. As long as it's about the giving back process, the sharing, the healing of the planet and of the people on it, the good of all concerned, the forces will be working on your side. So this is the step that's just about every morning taking fifteen minutes, first thing in the morning, to pray and meditate. To pray for the willingness to stay on the path, to pray for the willingness to receive the abundance that is coming, to pray for the exact vision that we're looking for, and also to meditate and allow our minds to rest, and allow the forces of the universe to work with us, to bring this stuff to us.

I heard Dr. Dwyer say on one of his audio tapes to kind of put it into an analogy of dreams, like in a dream state. Objects just come to you. You don't have to go to them. You could be having a dream and all of a sudden, something just appears in the dream, that's how this is. Just bring it to you and allow it to come. Accept it, be grateful, and thank the universe every day. And if you find it hard to do the gratitude and the thankfulness, I'd like to make a suggestion.

Every morning write ten things that you are grateful for, and they could be as simple as waking up, having eyes, having legs that work, having a house and roof over our heads, it could be that simple. But write down ten things every day until it's a natural state of being.

Gratitude. It's part of the manifesting process. It's part of the allowing process. It's part of the adage "like attracts like." Allow it to happen. Expect it to happen.

I want to wrap up with three more quotes. The first one is from *Daily Wisdom,* Buddhist inspirations:

> "June 4. Human intelligence is one of our problems, but it would be foolish to think that the solution is to reduce our intelligence. There is only one way out. We must not let our intelligence be guided by negative and harmful emotions. It must be guided only by proper and positive motivation if it is to become marvelously constructive."

The second reading is from *Reflections in the Light,* Shakti Gawain's daily meditations.

"June 4. Living your truth. From a deep quiet place begin to sense the life force within you. Imagine that you are following your own energy, feeling it, trusting it, moving with it in every moment of your life. You're being completely true to yourself, living and speaking your truth. You feel alive and empowered. Imagine that you are living your life fully and freely, and let yourself enjoy that experience. By being who you are and expressing yourself, you're having a healing and empowering effect on everyone you encounter and on the world around you." The meditation thought: *When I'm true to myself, I have a positive effect on the world around me.*

I want to close the book by giving you a daily affirmation that you can say to yourself. And I truly believe this about myself and about everyone else. "You are a perfect being. The universe loves you. You are created in perfection, by perfection, for perfection. Your success is guaranteed."

Love and Blessings,

With
Love and Light

Tami

For more information, personal coaching and events coming up, please check the website, *www.ihavethepower.us.*

Biography

Tami Friedman

. . . is devoted to freeing women from limiting beliefs that have held them back from achieving their full potential. Born in Brooklyn, Tami started her career at age 13 with her first sales job, was photographed for Avon's catalog when she was 16 and worked in the fashion industry as a showroom model. Her natural flair for fashion led her to found her own company Heartbreakers, after which she was asked to help start L.A. Gear Jeans, the only jeans line ever to be launched from a shoe business. She was pulling in $100,000 a year when the bottom fell out of her world. Success at a young age came with ill-advised business advisors that left her penniless. But she credits this period of her life with giving her the tools that eventually led her to realize her dreams.

She was literally living hand to mouth, but through hard work and the kindness of others, she began a new career. She studied for and passed the difficult exam for becoming a stock broker, and when she had learned the ropes on Wall Street, she attracted partnerships with wealthy clients during the prosperous Clinton-era. She purchased distressed real estate and used her creativity to renovate and rejuvenate the properties using Feng Shui to heal any defects in the energy and her eye for fashion to work on the interiors. She used her knowledge on Wall Street to judge the value of the properties, and her sense of numbers to know how to structure a deal.

With her new abundance under her own control this time, she was able to expand her horizons. In 2000, she became certified in hypnotherapy. Along the way, she also learned the benefits of daily meditation. She made pilgrimages to India to experience life in Tibetan Buddhist communities. She developed a stable spiritual practice for herself.

Gradually she was able to surpass the prosperity of her early adulthood, and have enough left over for the projects of her heart—caring for and rescuing animals and empowering others to manifest their goals in life. Her T.J. Friedman Fund rescued dogs and cats from death row, and today she is on the Board of Directors of Shelter Pet Alliance Organization so she is able to help shelters nationally. Her life coaching has helped people turn their lives around, transforming difficult situations into the realization of their dreams through their own efforts.

In her words, "Spirit is a big part of our lives. It's powerful." Tami believes that through meditation, we find the quiet person within us, we release the strong person within us, and through just being quiet, we are finally able to focus on our real desires. So often, the abundance we receive is directly related to our willingness to give to the projects closest to our hearts and allow it to come free of blocks.

Tami says, "People need to take risks to break away from unhealthy family and career situations, to look at their own skills and talents, and to apply them in ways that benefit themselves and others. You can't help anyone if you're on food stamps. And just money itself won't help. It's about finding your calling, and then having the courage to think well of yourself so you can go out and share it with the world."

Through her own experience, she knows this is especially true for women. "I see lots of other women who need to be given a chance to stand on their own feet, to believe in themselves—in success. It's been done for me, and I want to do it for as many others as I can. It's a kind of debt to the universe. It's the only debt that I have. And it's a good kind of debt."

I want to take a moment to invite you to spend time with me at a two day Seminar or one-on-one coaching agreement. You may call (845) 729-3728 or visit the website *www.Ihavethepower.us* and either myself or a staff member will be able to help you.

IMPORTANT DISCLAIMER

You are responsible for your own actions and your own life. I will give you all the tools I have used in my life for me to succeed and you must use them to the best of your ability.

Sometimes success happens very quickly for people because they are ready to receive abundance. Please do not let this discourage you from staying the course. Others can see results many years after doing these exercisers in this book.

The only thing that is for sure is that this book will help you see yourself bigger and better than you ever did and will give you many tools and ideas to help you achieve your dreams and goals.

I wish you all the best and may the angels and higher forces of light shine upon you in your journey to you highest dreams.

With Love
XOXOXO
Tami